Coloring Book for Adults and kids
Amazing Pigeon
Stress Relieving Designs for Adults
Relaxation

This ColoringBook Is Belongs To

____

____

____

TORONTO BOOKSTORE

Pigeons
Set

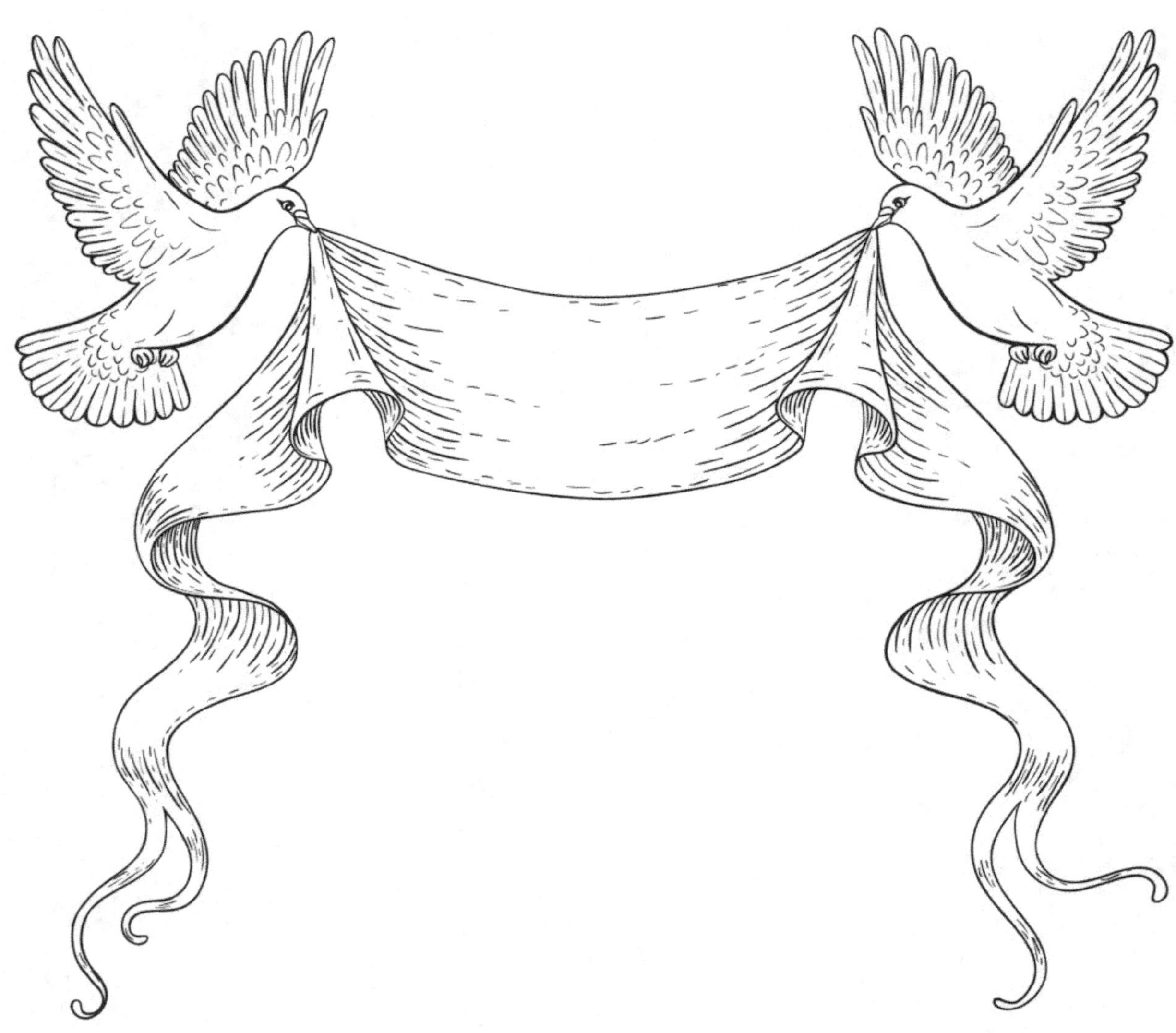

www.ingramcontent.com/pod-product-compliance
Lightning Source LLC
Chambersburg PA
CBHW081319250726
48662CB00008B/2643

9 798591 748807